Word Masala Award winners 2015

A Celebratory Collection

Word Masala Project Books
An imprint of Skylark Publications UK
In support of South-Asian diaspora writers and poets
10 Hillcross Avenue, Morden, Surrey SM4 4EA
www.skylarkpublications.co.uk

Front cover photograph courtesy of Lord Dholakia

We are also grateful to **Vipul Amin** for the use of his photographs
www.saypaneer.com

A Dipawali arrangement for the front cover and page 33
by **Sonal and Mrudang Patel**

© Yogesh Patel

First published in limited edition in December 2015

All rights reserved by the named contributors. No part of this publication may be reproduced, stored in a retrievable system or transmitted in any form or by any means, electronic, mechanical, photocopying, recording or otherwise without explicit permission from Yogesh Patel and the contributor.

Designed and printed in the UK

ISBN 978-0-9560840-3-3

Word Masala Award winners
2015
An anthology

Edited by

Yogesh Patel

Skylark Publications UK
London   New York

Word Masala Not-for-Profit Project

गुणाः पूजास्थानं

Good qualities are appreciated in whomsoever they are found.
Uttararaamacharitam (Bhavabhuti)

www.skylarkpublications.co.uk

Consultant Editor:

Dr Debjani Chatterjee MBE

Patrons

Prof Lord Bhikhu Parekh

Lord Dholakia, OBE DL

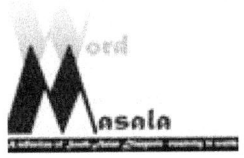

www.skylarkpublications.co.uk

गुणाः पूजास्थानं

Good qualities are appreciated in whomsoever they are found.
Uttararaamacharitam (Bhavabhuti)

Director: Yogesh Patel

Suite 6, Riverside House, 196 Wandle Road, Morden, Surrey SM4 6AU, England

---

Word Masala Awards are one year young now, but still very ambitious.

History

Skylark has published international contemporary poetry in translation since 1969. We ceased publishing in print after its 100th issue. Many illustrious names have featured in Skylark, including **Jorge Luis Borges (Argentina), Pablo Neruda, Norman Hidden (UK), Amrita Pritam & Shivkumar Batalvi (India), Peter Paul Wiplinger (Austria),** and **Dr Wazir Aga (Pakistan).** Its co-editor, and poet, Yogesh Patel, founded Skylark Publications UK with a view to *helping Diasporic and expat writers.* We have just begun a journey. After one year, we struggle like all other small magazines and small press. But it has not deterred them, nor will it us.

From its outset Lord Dholakia, Lord Parekh and Dr Debjani Chatterjee have helped it as patrons. *Being a very active supporter Debjani has moved to the position of Consultant Editor* to allow her to make a more valuable contribution. Our focus is on helping South-Asian diasporic and expat authors and poets. With that in mind, after the first **printed volume of Word Masala** in 2011, we have now very successfully published **eSkylark as an e-zine, along with the printed and the web versions.** The magazine brings a poet or a poem at least once a month to our very large worldwide readership. We also highlight news, book launches, events, markets and other opportunities which help our readers.

Some of our aims

1. Once a month we bring a poem by a poet from the South-Asian diaspora and present a brief bio-data. **'Poets of the month'** are vetted and selected by a team comprising of our previous award winners, editor and patrons. This award is only by invitation. We also plan to bring diasporic poetry in **Translation** to the attention of readers.
2. **A reader's critique in 50 words** for the poem appearing in the previous issue will be considered for publication in the next issue with a credit and writer's brief bio-data. Submissions for this are open to all, not just to diaspora poets. The aim is to allow an interaction with poets and writers from both inside and outside the diaspora. So you are welcome to send such critique with your bio-data, but strictly within these limitations.
3. Sadly, we have yet to find **Poetry Films** by poets from the Indian sub-continent. We encourage poets to explore this genre and let us have links to their work. This feature is open to **all Indic language poets anywhere** and all are encouraged to let us have such links. Please note we WILL NOT accept a link to other websites involved in similar activities. YouTube, Hotmail, Google or Dropbox types of storage links or links to your own web pages are acceptable.
4. We aim to organise a **Poetry Presentation** by our award winners once a year **at the House of Lords**. This may happen at the House of Lords at the discretion of Lord Parekh and other supporting peers.
5. Currently, **the organisations we work with** are the Gujarati Literary Academy UK, the Healing Word, the High Commission of India in London, Vatayan, Asian Voice newspapers, the Yunus Emre Turkish Cultural Centre, the Nehru Centre, and the Poetry Library.
6. We aim to create **an archive of audios** by diaspora poets.
7. We aim to **provide a web link to books by our readers and poets**. Please send your books to our postal address.
8. If you are a published poet or author, please inform us **if you are willing to review** books. This feature is open to everyone.
9. Our list includes **libraries**, and **we encourage them** to explore and buy the books from the list that we put forward.
10. Please inform us of your literary events

Contents

Word Masala Award Winners

Shanta Acharya
In a Time of Siege	16
London: 7th July 2005	17
Christmas Gifts	25
Boxing Day	26
Fever in Diwali	36

Usha Akella
A Lot of Light Because…	13
Lemon Basil	20
Computer Sky	21
One	22
The Season Passes	37

Meena Alexander
Field in Summer	14
Kabir Sings…	8
Inwood Sita	28
Lyric Ego	40
Dwelling	40

Debjani Chatterjee
This Truth	15
Christmas	22
Victoria's Statue	28
Diwali	30
Heart Tanka	30
Lotus Meditation	31
UN Observer	31
The Great Houdini	31
Winter Tanka	40

Usha Kishore
From Hatred to Love	14
Ganesh Utsav	27
Sari	39
Waiting for Autumn	41

Reginald Massey
An Image	35
We'd Never Know	35
Lover Come Late	35

Daljit Nagra
Our Town….	34

Saleem Peeradina
In Praise of Persimmons	23
A Paean to the Papaya	29
Pineapple	38
Sisters	43
From Meditation on Desire	44

Editorial Contribution

Yogesh Patel
Namaste	Back Cover
A Drought Deciduous…	10
(On a photograph by Lord Dholakia)	
The Poor People of Paris	12
(An Editorial Tribute to Paris Victims)	

WMP Award Winner

Sweta Vikram
Ghazal	45

Introduction

Namasté to all Word Masala Award winners 2015 and *namasté* from our winners to readers of eSkylark during 2015! Each poet displays considerable talent. This collection does not pretend to offer a representative work by these poets in any sense. Its focus, as would be the case with most anthologies, is limited in scope. It celebrates the spirit of Diwali and Christmas 2015, as well as the success of Word Masala Award winners of the year. Hopefully, it will bring their achievements yet again to the attention of publishers, editors, libraries and event organisers, to allow them to be more inclusive of BAME talent.

Word Masala Project began in 2011, but its path did not become too clear until January 2015 when eSkyalrk was launched, following discussion that took place throughout 2014. We listed many objectives in our first e-zine that reached a large readership. We were encouraged by the fact that an overwhelming majority wished to support our venture. Today, after one year, we are moving from strength to strength, not only in numbers but, also in actual achievements by South-Asian diaspora writers and poets. So, many activities such as reviews, books accepted for publication, prizes, media exposure, and events come to mind. A snub, once offered at the start of this project, is receding fast.

Sadly, one or two diaspora poets, here and there, who have been highly successful in joining the literary establishment, and have perhaps avoided being closely identified with the diaspora, are serving well those who still reject BAME talent. The successful sometimes forget their early struggles and their roots, and are seduced by money.

When small presses like Valley Press and larger publishers like Faber and Faber step forward to be supportive, optimism is no longer a glass half empty. This project salutes them. *Many magazine editors still have a very long way to go in supporting BAME talent!* Publishing can be a strange place: many mainstream publishers in the UK open offices in India to make money, while disappointing and ignoring the diaspora writers who are right here! Perhaps there is a point of debate regarding the different styles of presentation and subject matter that diaspora poets may be offering. Word Masala Project aims to be a bridging activity to encourage editors, publishers, event organisers and diaspora poets. Our work at Word Masala is to facilitate a meeting of minds and help proven diaspora poets to build their brands, which is regrettably so utterly ignored by the poetry establishment in the UK!

This year in America, our Award Winner Usha Akella, who is a Cultural Ambassador of the City of Austin, successfully launched a major poetry festival, Matwaala, for diaspora poets in the USA. Word Masala Award winner Saleem Peeradina was also instrumental in organising it. Valley Press, mentioned above, plan to publish his latest collection in June 2016, a work that is much anticipated. With such international successes, Word Masala is well placed to progress satisfactorily in 2016.

Now we have clearly set out a threefold approach: Word Masala Project, with its awards, variety of activities and impact as a recognised force; Skylark Publications UK, subsidising the project and providing a print vehicle like crowdfunding for poet Mona Dash's planned anthology; and eSkylark, an e-zine and printed magazine.

Hence, from January 2016, as our new program goes forth with Awards, it will be published with its own ISSN, ISSN 2397-1878.

It is also intended that Skylark magazine will be resurrected to promote poetry in translation from diaspora poets and expatriate poets writing in their own languages, an area of writing almost totally ignored by publishers. They make a very valuable contribution in their own languages in the countries of their adoption. As befitting its ethos, Skylark magazine will revive its new journey as ISSN 0257-3857.

We are very much mindful of the fact that poetry is not a big business and so many small press publishers struggle to no end while they carry on publishing out of a passion for poetry. We at Word Masala just want to tap into that passion with a positive attitude.

Enjoy the collection!

Yogesh Patel

We welcome your comments and support. Please join the list.
1. Please buy the merchandise to help. See our shop at www.skylarkpublictions.co.uk
2. Please subscribe to our crowdfunding projects for the books
3. Please DONATE
4. Please buy our books and the books by our recommended poets
5. Please spread the word about us in your social media
6. PLEASE REVIEW AND PUBLISH OUR DIASPORA POETS
7. Please invite them to events and festivals for the readings and talks.

Yogesh Patel

A Drought Deciduous Gaze
(Sparked by a photograph by Lord Dholakia)

The days you look at
Has no ahead, a barren hope
But a hope indeed
The drifting dry bush
The dust, the sand
But the determination is hope
A few drops of rain
Wakes up the crop, named tomorrow
So, I carry an axe
To cut out the stubborn
Thorny strangling weeds
And let the seeds
Meet the next day

Hence, don't look at the grazed
Landscape on my face

Editor: Although this is a festive issue, we think it entirely appropriate to include a special section of poems by Word Masala Award winning poets to pay tribute to so many who lost their lives in the madness of November 2015 in Paris and elsewhere in the world.

A tribute to victims of the Paris massacre

Yogesh Patel

The Poor People of Paris

Wipe I will not
tears, dews
from the cheeks of
roses, carnations and tulips
in the morning after
when I had to dip the nib
into thickened black blood
to write my song
at the oblivious sunrise
witnessing hugs of strangers
hands and palms locked
to fill sun's absence

Crow* stood victorious!

The free tea from a café
was warmer than the sun
as it defied camouflaged robots
blind to Asimov's third law

I listen to the lone pianist
emerging from nowhere
who sits and plays
Night and day they're making music
While they're making love in French
The poor people of Paris

The poor people of Paris
The kind that blunts Kalashnikov
The poor people of Paris**

* Refers to crow's revolt in *Crow: From the Life and Songs of the Crow* by Ted Hughes
***A classic Jack Lawrence song*

(An editorial tribute)

Usha Akella

A Lot of Light Because It was Like a Concert

So much breaking news everybody is broken,
Who wakes up whole when the sun rises?
Let me know, learn to twist your tongue in new names
to count history's footsteps: Tenancingo/
Abdelhamid Abaaoud/ Aulnay-sous-Bois/
Hasna Ait Boulahcen/Bataclan/ Bernard Cazeneuve.
Know boys will be boys and the clan is the clan,
And we will strengthen our borders to keep the madness in,
And Justin Bieber can end a show after one song,
And Karla is raped 43,200 times four years long,
And who has the true religion in this gallimaufry?
Explain it any way you can- this our earth, turquoise marble in
a pristine mind coming undone, perhaps
the clash between yin and yang, the apogee and perigee of sin,
While the officials take their papillary prints and
some are sure someone measures the soul's thumbprint,
And someone can say of carnage:
"And a lot of light because it was like a concert."
Go figure that.

The captain of the commandos, who wanted to be known only as Jeremy, told NBC News he entered the theatre to find several hundred people lying motionless on the floor, not making a sound, "because they were afraid of the terrorist."
"Tons of bloods everywhere. No sound," he said. "Nobody was screaming ... and a lot of light because it was like a concert." – Network Writer News Corp Australia Network, Newscom.au

Usha Kishore

From Hatred to Love

*I held an atlas in my lap
ran my fingers across the whole world
and whispered
where does it hurt?*
              (Warsan Shire)

Spiralling through the city's rib cage,
snaking across its districts, across
the world, without logic or reason,
a fire of hatred spreads. It hurts everywhere.
A wound pierces the heart of the earth,
that no words can fill.
What made this fire?
Was it water, air or sky?
What crimes of empires, of people
of lost worlds, will this fire burn?
Drown this fire in song,
rouse the world from darkness
to light, from hatred to love.

Meena Alexander

Field in Summer

I had a simple childhood,
A mother and father to take care of me,
no war at my doorstep.

Stones sang
canticles in my mouth
as darkness rose.

Love, love where are they gone?
Father, mother, ink dark stars,
singing stones.

Debjani Chatterjee

This Truth

Revolution raged.
Liberté, égalité,
et fraternité.

Paris and Mumbai,
London, New York, all cities...
the price that we pay...

Heads roll, bullets fire;
life is cheap for terrorists -
especially theirs.

United we grow.
Now *nous somme Parisienne.*
World map rewritten.

This Truth will prevail:
liberté, égalité,
et fraternité

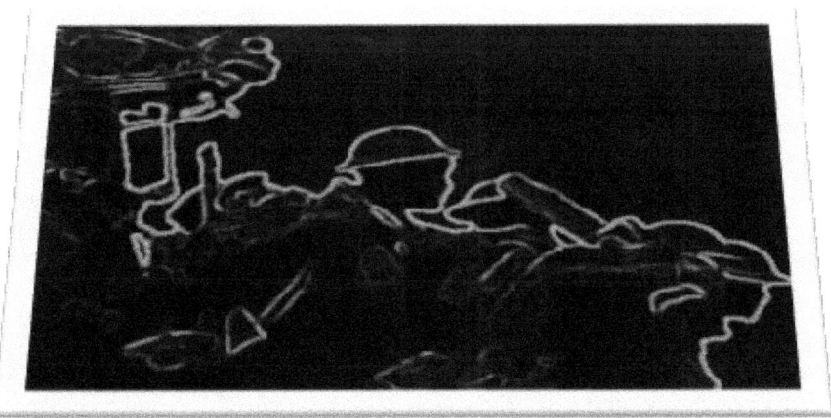

Shanta Acharya

In a Time of Siege
(Paris: 13 November 2015)

How does one learn to love in a time of siege?
My days, locked in, are incoherent with fear,
nightmares usurp my peace.

I keep seeing the same scenes over and over –
in the concert hall we are swaying to the music,
mistaking gunshots for fireworks.

In an instant we get a grip on reality,
guns already pumping blood on the floor –
unprepared were we for this brutal awakening.

Bodies bursting with life moments ago
now lie inert, wearing death masks, on the floor –
as if we are in some Theatre of the Absurd,
transformed unwittingly into characters on a stage.
Except this is real – you sprawled on me,
protecting me with your last breath.

I cannot stop shivering,
your still-warm blood splattered all over –
the weight of your body steadying me.
In my nightmare I hear only screaming,
wake up in a sweat, howling …

We knew the world had its problems,
everywhere there is pain and suffering.

How can adding to human misery make things better?
Not all's fair in love and war, remember –

Life's a spell so exquisite,
everything conspires to break it.

Tell me of love and hope, of hearts that endure.
This universe, my love, lives and grows inside us,
the world outside is forever diminishing to nothing.

Shanta Acharya

London: 7th July 2005

Flash of yellow light, blinding
the splinter of glass in my eye –
then silence as if thunder had lost its calling,
the brain's beating tide of blood drumming…

People wearing fear on their faces
like protective masks
mouths distorted, screaming,
came pouring out of the tunnel –
stumbling over bodies lying
in the Underground station,
some unaware of limbs missing.
Is this our 9/11, terror unfolding?

Unable to protect myself from danger
(I had marched against the war)
I lay paralysed on the bloodied floor
each cell in me a survivor…

Who would not rather live –
          with or without a god?

Trapped in hell, my thoughts were of you,
my children, and you whom I hold dear.

Clinging to hope in a dark, cold corner,
fist wrapped tight round an angel's finger,
no stranger my knight in shining armour,
          my valiant fire fighter.

Meena Alexander

(Reprinted from the New Yorker in the aftermath of 9/11)

Kabir Sings in a City of Burning Towers

What a shame
they scared you so
you plucked your sari off,
crushed it into a ball

then spread it
on the toilet floor.
Sparks from the towers
fled through the weave of silk.

With your black hair
and sun dark skin
you're just a child of earth.
Kabir the weaver sings:

O men and dogs
in times of grief
our rolling earth
grows small.

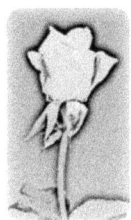

Celebratory Poems

Usha Akella

Lemon Basil

How close you hold her pressing her
into your side,
leg against leg—she isn't your wife.
I wondered about that one,

and how you spilled your books like a schoolboy
while I stoically sipped tea
in a buttoned up jacket of rust (covered like a nun.)

(Your dog lay at my feet bewitched,
the cat glided by, I was uncertain
what to do with the dog's devotion.)

It matched the flaming bushes out there,
You plucked a leaf, held it against my sleeve
and said, "Almost."

We walked through the herb garden
and forests painting the sky yellow,
I stumbled .You caught my arm. Pressed it.

I did not ignite. The house was the colour of my dreams.
For weeks the world smelt of the lemon basil
crumpled into a notebook.

Later, the poems completed what I could not,
Almost. Love must be conjured up when it is not.

Usha Akella

Computer Sky

Dark space deep as a well,
long before we met what was ours
was a bird—a dove, I would think,
So when we met we had already
flown away, and the rustle of that flight
lay between us; a wingspan of peace.
Two banks—we run along
the river, at the edge of ours

Usha Akella

One

My pen skips too easily to write another alphabet,
of another time—quills, blue skies, the flight of birds,
woods and lakes, walking, always walking even before
we walked, so when we walk now Life is memory.
How do I know a Time before this time?
Easily, the past quietly rows itself on the lake of the
present, And your eyes still—all Time in them.

I watch myself as a gladiator watches his moves
drawn to his opponent, his altar—quietly. This one
teaches me patience. When is the lake still?
When it perfectly embraces the tree at its edge,
transposed without a tremor, one lake, one tree, one.

Debjani Chatterjee

Christmas

The yawning year rubs sleepy eyes
As Mercy's shawl falls from the skies -
A birth-blanket like a blessing.

Crystals sparkle in cool crisp air,
The world is Christmas white and fair –
Hope's message to all addressing.

Saleem Peeradina

In Praise of Persimmons

Celebrated in Chinese and Japanese art, the persimmon
Grows in clumps on a canopy of branches. It is routinely

Pecked by parrots, nibbled by fat ants, filched
By monkeys. Its smooth, orange skin distinguishes it

From its look alike, the tomato. But what sets it apart
Is the dry, curly, brittle, four-leaf top it wears for headcover.

The persimmon is for those who are in no hurry to attack
The fruit. Like a hard kiwi, eat it too soon

When it is not ripe, and your mouth will protest. With a hard
Persimmon, the inside of your mouth will turn chalky.

You have to wait until the fruit decides it is ready.
Then its astringency will have faded, and it will reward

Your patience by yielding its soft, velvety flesh
With a sweetness matched only by your memory of mangoes.

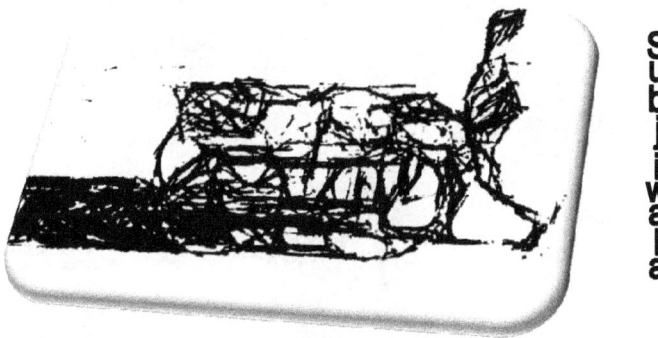

Subjiwala

A Child Santa

Shanta Acharya

Christmas Gifts

The morning sun burst forth excitedly –
a child drawing the curtains in the sea-sky
of cumulus clouds, climbing crazily

over rooftops to be the first to greet me,
cajole me out of bed to marvel at a world
gift wrapped with snow, especially for me.

The scene is pure white, silent lace
spread over sleepy rooftops, smoking chimneys
and TV aerials, the antenna antlers of trees.

The wind has taken leave for the day,
having departed with its musical tattoo
it so loves to practice on my rickety windows.

Last night as I celebrated midnight mass live
from Westminster Cathedral, courtesy of the BBC,
with tidings of joy from the Adventist chorale on ITV,

the wind conducted its own inimitable ceremony
beating the drums of fate on the Victorian glass
of my windows, touched by a wild full-moon ecstasy.

I have learnt in my life to cherish the gifts of fate.
Ave Maria! Agnus Dei! Veni Sancte Spiritus –

The afternoon sun kindly offered to unwrap my gift for me.
The hours invited me for communion in Highgate Wood

with the squirrels and robins, blackbirds and crows.
The pigeons and dogs greeted each other, not forgetting me.

There were human faces too wrapped in winter.
My neighbours could not stop for me but the royal trees'
Christmas message was prepared especially for me.

Shanta Acharya

Boxing Day

The full moon rose like an aria in the sky,
my thoughts, a flock of geese, fly homewards.

The landline hums with voices of my little nephews and nieces
assuring me all's well with the world –

Their vowels travelling excitedly over
windswept clouds, buoyed across continents,
carrying the joys of the universe in their drift,
showering me with armful of gifts.

No longer cold and restless like the temple monkeys in Puri,
I watch the snow scatter the darkness of my soul.
Through the window I stare at stars shining steadfastly.

All children are messengers of hope.
I remember the words of my grandfather
uttered in a moment of grace and lucidity.

Old age arrives with no warning,
bringing with it disease, dependence, suffering.

Crossing the boundary between human and divine,
my spirit swirls like music.

Christ, Krishna or Ganesha, are as much my endowment
as all the children who sleep hungry tonight.

Usha Kishore

Ganesh Utsav

Come immerse yourself in my tears,
elephant boy, let me gather the sighs
that flower in my mind and adorn your feet.

All day long, milling crowds gather
in whirling thoughts, bells ring
in the wind, conches blow in the waves
and a fragrance rises in the mists.

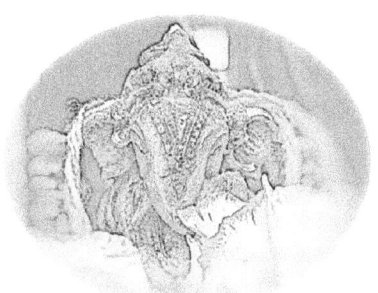

Let me dip my heart in camphor
and light it to illumine your face.
Let my prayers fly down as autumn
leaves and scent your hands.

Caught between light and dark, living
in the aesthetic of nowhere, my verse
loses its rhythm. All alone, I stand
on a distant shore, with a bowlful
of *kheer* to tickle your elephant tastes.

Come Ganesha, bathe in the Irish Sea...

Ganesh Utsav - is the festival of the Hindu Elephant God, Ganesh or Ganesha. After a week of prayer and festivities, the idol of Ganesh is immersed in the sea or in a body of water.
Camphor - an inflammable plant resin used in Hindu worship.
Kheer - Hindi for milk pudding

Meena Alexander

Inwood Sita

Sita bathed in sand.
By wildwort
And willowherb
Fire starts—

Dry ground cracks,
Swallows her whole.
Sita- found- in- a- field
Fled to Inwood.

Rama cast her out,
Lava storms cooled her
Dirt cloaked her,
A shimmering stole.

Days later, on Dyckman Street
As cobbles crack
She slips into a manhole,
Waves at me.

Debjani Chatterjee

Victoria's Statue

It amused Queen Victoria
To be Empress of India
Although she never travelled there,
She left her statue everywhere.

Saleem Peeradina

A Paean to the Papaya

There were two kinds of papaya trees in the backyard
Of my childhood: the ones that bore a spray of flowers
And others that were stacked with green fruit. It was my first
Lesson in Horticulture: papaya trees, my mother would say,
Come in two genders – neuter and female.

Slice open a ripe papaya from stem to stern and you'll find
A boatload of black, peppery, pellets. Scrape these out
And take in the colors of this fruit which may range
From yellow to orange to blushing pink. Then cut out the thick
Peel, cube the flesh, and taste its sweetness melt in your mouth.

Raw papaya pickle was among the variety of pickles made
By the women in the family. Diced papaya was combined with
Sliced carrot, fresh ginger and turmeric, seasoned with
Mustard and soaked in vinegar, then bottled for daily use.
It was a strong, sour, salty, crunchy blend that puckered
My mouth, but for which I developed a taste only later in life.

Debjani Chatterjee

Diwali

Diwali lamps are twinkling, twinkling
In the sky and in our homes and hearts.
We welcome all with cheery greetings
And sweets and patterned *rangoli* art.
Lakshmi flies upon her owl tonight;
Incense curls, our future's sparkling bright.

Heart Tanka

Goddess, your lac-dyed
feet once danced upon my sigh.
When the heart's lava
flowed, I dipped both hands in red
and splashed it across the sky.

Kali, I have found
the hibiscus at your feet
is the red flower
of your divine forgiveness.
I give it with each heartbeat.

Debjani Chatterjee

Lotus Meditation

Behold the lotus
blooming in muddy water,
pure and radiant.

UN Observer

A UN observer, Dr Smith had come
to see which nation was being troublesome.
So, when thrown off the plane, he was rather glad,
for the view looked clearer and his sight was bad.

The Great Houdini

The Great Houdini,
like a mysterious genie,
vanished during his final act,
thus creating both legend and fact.

Meena Alexander

Bright Passage

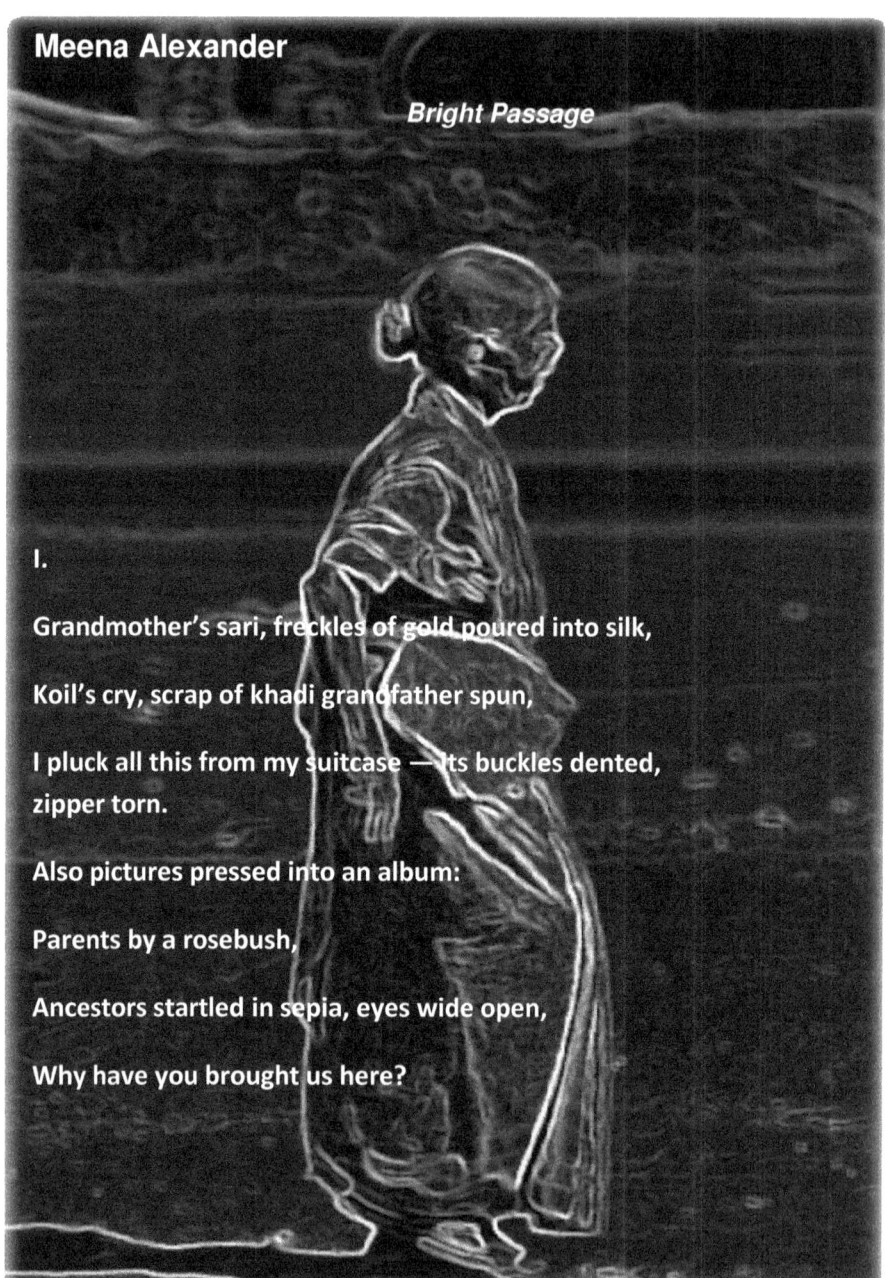

I.

Grandmother's sari, freckles of gold poured into silk,

Koil's cry, scrap of khadi grandfather spun,

I pluck all this from my suitcase —its buckles dented, zipper torn.

Also pictures pressed into an album:

Parents by a rosebush,

Ancestors startled in sepia, eyes wide open,

Why have you brought us here?

II.

Mist soars on the river, my door splits free of its hinges:
My children's children, and those I will never see –
Generations swarm in me,
Born to this North American soil, dreamers in a new world.
I must pass through that rocking doorway,
Figure out words, clean minted, untranslatable –
Already in the trees finches are warbling, calling my name.

Note: *This poem was specially composed for the exhibit Beyond Bollywood: Indian Americans Shape the Nation, Smithsonian, Washington DC, 2014-2015. The first stanza of the poem appears on the wall of the exhibit just as you enter, above a trunk filled with various articles a migrant might have brought with her. (Published in India Quarterly, 2014)*

Daljit Nagra

Our Town with the Whole of India!

Our town in England with the whole of India sundering
out of its temples, mandirs and mosques for the customised
streets. Our parade, clad in cloak-orange with banners
and tridents, chanting from station to station for Vasaikhi
over Easter. Our full moon madness for Eidh with free
pavement tandooris and legless dancing to boostered
cars. Our Guy Fawkes' Diwali - a kingdom of rockets
for the Odysseus-trials of Rama who arrowed the jungle
foe to re-palace the Penelope-faith of his Sita.

(Due to the copyright restrictions, please read the full poem at our website: www.skylarkpublications.co.uk)

Reginald Massey

An Image

The autumn moon
Willow-veiled,
Beckons her silent love
The pool:
For she knows
His patient eyes
Will soon be glazed
With a cataract
Of ice.

We'd Never Know

In the afternoon
The sky-sketching hawks
Draw invisible lines.
Their work may be great,
May be consummate;
But we'd never know
The artistry
Of hawk, pigeons, sparrows, or crow

Lover Come Late

The spring, like lovers will, comes late.
Feels guilty and makes
An unceremonious dash
The cherry tree, frozen from waiting
All winter, blushes
And is soon covered in a pink rash

Shanta Acharya

Fever in Diwali

Pious neighbours celebrated Diwali
with neat rows of oil lamps
promising the destruction of evil.

My fever flew fast through the coil of night
setting ablaze the desolate sky
like a child conspiring with confetti stars.

Harassed doctors came with tablets,
magic, miniature moons
with syrup in exorcist cups and hermetic brew.

While the snake-charmer's fluted thermometer
grinned its flinted fangs wider and wider,
I ate moons and laughed at stars.

My limbs could've even danced a few steps to appease
evil with the grace of lightning in a storm ripped sky
like blue throated Shiva with snakes in red matted hair.

White sheeted, I lay still
like an Indian monkey in summer.

The audio of this poem is available at our website: www.skylarkpublications.co.uk

Usha Akella

The Season Passes

Know this; you make me write poetry,
I who feel much like a blank page
move to fill myself with words,

Know too: I ache at times to tell
you of our similarities, that
I know your soul as a page might

know a poem, and is still
till it is filled. Is now the time?
I stir and fall back into reticence,

knowing the season will pass.
I ask only this—are you by the window
aware of the empty space by you?

Saleem Peeradina

Pineapple

Although clad in armor with eyes all over its body looking
As if it is keeping watch, it lowers its gaze when

You meet it. The pity is-- in order to reach its fleshy
Interior, you have to be so violent to this peaceful fruit:

Lop off its crown of thorns, slice the bottom flat, then
Gouge its eyes out as you proceed to take off its armor.

Discard the hard cylindrical core if you prefer, quarter it
Or halve it length-wise, cut circles, or cubes, or sticks

Or shred it, depending on where it is going – salad,
Shake, sherbet, cake, custard. The golden ones are

The sweetest. On a hot day, you can count on its juice
To quench your thirst and calm your insides like citrus

Fruit does. Strangely, its acidity can tame a greasy meal.
Its fragrance alone can make some people happy.

Usha Kishore

Sari

Batiqued ethnic desires
wax dyed by the sun
on the earth's longest fabric,
the sky, where words lose
themselves in clouds,
like a river, it tumbles
from the astral zone,
translating myth
and legend that burn
on the fires of chant and hymn,
wafting in frangipani
and jasmine, waxing
and waning like the moon,
falling across time
like unending trails
of thought, in a metaphor
of rain, a lightning torsade
stolen from passing monsoons,
clinging to the fingertips
like a lingering memory,
a long strip of silk
that stretches
across continents,
my *sari* is a dream
of border crossings,
the remains of a culture
treasured in a dark corner
of the mind's wardrobe.

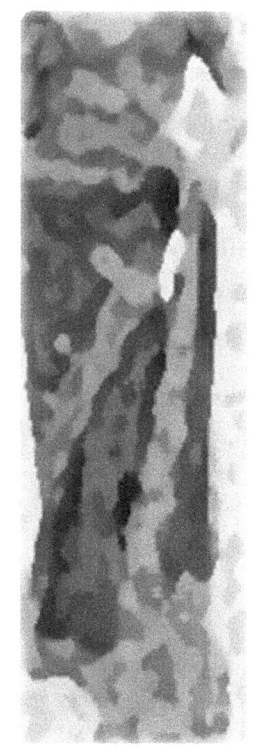

Meena Alexander

Lyric Ego

Muslin and lavender
Under mosquito nets,
Nothing to hold – just drops of blood
From an ancestral sword.

Dwelling

Where the ground shakes
I set my tent.
We cannot know ourselves ever.
I write this on your sleeve,
Fold the cotton over.
Sweet sunlight—
What swans found
In their last flight.

Debjani Chatterjee

Winter Tanka

A white fleece blankets
The sleeping earth while snowdrops
Dream spring hosannas.
And icicle prayer-flags
Hibernate on bare branches.

Usha Kishore

Waiting for Autumn

Autumn, you are the beginning and the end.
Leaves of burgeoned gold flirt with the sky
in burnt ochre, sprinkling *sindoor* into my thoughts
as darkness invades light, charms her and makes her
his paramour. The colours of spring are too pastel
and summer is dyed, far too often, in shades of grey.
But, you Autumn, queen of seasons, eternal bride
of the sun, dressed in russet red, edged with burnished
gold, erupt into song and kiss my soul. You warm me
with your soft fires as the sky turns into birds
and chases a fleeing summer. Then I, the dark woman,
in the trajectory of your consciousness, echo your dreams…

Your dark days dance like peacocks and call out
in monsoon klaxon. Your winds strum home-thoughts
in the notes of a thousand *vinas*. Your crimson waters
bleed into the earth, your womb bursts open in coral
and fills the air with mellow mists. When I become
broody, you lend me your womb…

Your rain-clouds gather, hiding *Indra's* lightning bow,
bearing the rumbling message of a *Yaksha*, lost
in a mountain kingdom. You ripen my verse
with the melodies of the plains and hills you soar
on your wings. Take my melancholy in return,
scatter it in your insides, to sprout in your fields
and harvest it in golden sheaves…

I hear your laughter rustling through the night; hail
stones, your broken bangles, speak of spent passion
with the sleeping sun. Your glittering frost, jewels
for the trees, pours from the red sky like the tears
of an exile. Your moon, cloaked in mists, serenades

my *chakora* spirit with fragrant madrigals

and leaves his rays on the edge of my *sari*.
When the wintry hordes attack, you break
into gold, red and amber and immolate yourself
in endless spaces, and time freezes in my veins.
But I know, you will rise again like the phoenix.
Until then, Autumn, I shall wait for you...

Sindoor Sindoor - red powder worn on the forehead
Vina - Stringed musical instrument
Yaksha - Indian demi-god
Chakora - partridge. In Indian folklore, the chakora is in love with the moon.
{Acknowledging the works of the legendary Sanskrit poet, Kalidasa}

Saleem Peeradina

Sisters

One, not quite ten
but ahead of the other, younger
whose five plus will never catch up
with the big one's lead
no matter how good she acts
or how hard she cheats.

Like any disadvantaged species
she has turned the handicap
in her favor: she's bolder,
sneakier, sweeter than honey,
obeyer of commands, underminer of rules,
producer of tears, yeller, complete

Turnaround. The older gets
the tough end of it. Most times
blames end up in her sullen face.
Fighting back, she argues, attacks
me for taking the wrong side.
I sweet-talk her the way all parents

At all times have tried explaining
to the elder child. Living up
to her inheritance, she blazes back
at my moralizing. On bad days
I shout her down, immediately
regretting my words.

But even as she retreats
into a simmering silence, she stands her ground
knowing me to be unfair. Secretly,
I rejoice at the lesson never intended
but so well learnt: how to overcome
fathers, real and imagined.

Saleem Peeradina

From **Meditation on Desire**

    1

I can never say
What I feel about you.
Listen hard
for syllables unspoken,
not yet formed.
As for words
that do surface,
frisk them thoroughly
before inviting them in.

    2
Framed as I am
by convention, what can I do
but cast a cold eye
on the line
I cannot breach,
cannot shift,
cannot undraw.

    3
Only in the abstract
can words attain
such luminosity.
On contact
with the flesh
they burn up.

    4
You give my words
an eager ear
thereby
planting in my tongue
a false hope.

Sweta Vikram

Ghazal

Dear husband: try to leave your scent behind.

Eyes follow me around,
asking me to wash
my muddy toes dirtied by the rain.
They say red
doesn't belong in my hair.
The voices of your children
I recognize as they call me names.
I sing in silence.
I wonder
if my shadow will be mine
after you are gone.

Dear husband: try to leave your scent behind.

I know
your *Old Spice* on my pillowcase
will drive me insane.
The music made
with our morning laughter
will forever haunt
my ghazals.
My tongue will burn
from wanting to kiss
the *Old Monk* breath
and words of love on your dark lips.

Dear husband: try to leave your scent behind.

Award Winning Poets

Bio

 **Debjani Chatterjee**

Delhi-born Debjani Chatterjee grew up in India, Japan, Bangladesh, Hong Kong, Egypt and Morocco, and now lives in Sheffield. She has written and edited over 65 books, including *Namaskar: New & Selected Poems* and *Monkey King's Party*.

She is a Patron of Survivors' Poetry, Life Member of the Poetry Society in India and the UK, and founder of The Healing Word.

A former Royal Literary Fund Fellow, Chair of the National Association of Writers in Education and the Arts Council of England's Translations Panel, she has held writing residencies at Sheffield Children's Hospital and York St John and Leeds Trinity universities.

She has won many major prizes. She received an honorary doctorate from Sheffield Hallam University in 2002 and an MBE in 2008.

www.debjanichatterjee.moonfruit.com

 **Daljit Nagra**

Daljit Nagra comes from a Punjabi background. He was born and raised in London, then Sheffield. He has won several prestigious prizes for his poetry. In 2004, he won the Forward Prize for Best Individual Poem with *Look We Have Coming to Dover!* This was also the title of his first collection which was published by Faber & Faber in 2007. This won the South Bank Show Decibel Award, the Forward Prize for Best First Collection and was nominated for The Costa Prize, The Guardian First Book Prize, the Aldeburgh Prize and the Glen Dimplex Award. His second collection, *Tippoo Sultan's Incredible White-Man Eating Tiger-Toy Machine!!!* was shortlisted for the TS Eliot Prize. His current book, *Ramayana*, is shortlisted for the TS Eliot Prize. In 2014 he won the Royal Society of Authors Travelling Scholarship Award.

Daljit's poems have been published in *New Yorker, Atlantic Review, London Review of Books, Times Literary Supplement, Poetry Review, Poetry London, Poetry International, Rialto* and *The North*.

Daljit has been on the Board of the Poetry Book Society and the Poetry Archive. He has judged the Samuel Johnson Award 2008, The Guardian First Book Prize 2008, The Foyles Young Poets Competition 2008, The National Poetry Competition 2009, the Costa Poetry category and the overall winner in 2012. He has also hosted the TS Eliot Poetry Readings 2009. He is the Keats' House Poet-In-Residence from July 2014 – June 2015, and he was an Eton College Wisdom Scholar in November 2014. He is the Lead Poetry Tutor at The Faber Academy and has run workshops all over the world. He is a regular contributor to *BBC radio and has written articles for The Financial Times, The Guardian, The Observer, The Times of India*.

 **Meena Alexander**

Meena Alexander's eighth book of poetry *Atmospheric Embroidery* has just been published in India (New Delhi, Hachette India, 2015). Her works include the PEN Award winning book of poems *Illiterate Heart*, and *Birthplace with Buried Stones* (published by TriQuarterly Books/Northwestern University Press). She is the author of the critically acclaimed memoir *Fault Lines* (one of *Publishers Weekly's* Best Books of the Year.

She has also published two novels; two books of essays on poetics and two academic studies. She is the editor of *Indian Love Poems* (Knopf/Everyman's Library). Her poems have been widely translated and set to music, most recently by the Swedish composer Jan Sandstrom, performed in Stockholm by the Serikon Music Ensemble and the Swedish Radio Choir. Her awards include those from the John Simon Guggenheim Foundation, Fulbright Foundation, Arts Council of England and the Rockefeller Foundation for a residency at Bellagio. In 2014 she was named a National Fellow at the Indian Institute of Advanced Study, Shimla. She is Distinguished Professor of English, Graduate Center/ Hunter College, CUNY.

www.meenaalexander.com

Saleem Peeradina

Saleem Peeradina is the author of *First Offence* (Newground, 1980), *Group Portrait* (OUP, 1992),*Meditations on Desire* (Ridgeway Press, 2003), and *Slow Dance* (Ridgeway Press, 2010). He edited *Contemporary IndianPoetry in English* (Macmillan, 1972), one of the earliest and most widely
used texts in courses on South Asian literature. *The Ocean in My Yard*, a prose memoir of growing up in Bombay, was published by Penguin Books, in 2005. A new collection of poetry, *Final Cut,* awaits publication. *Meditations on Desire* was recently published in Arabic translation by Kalima Publishers in Abu Dhabi, UAE.

His poetry is represented in most major anthologies of Indian, South Asian, and Asian American writing including *The Oxford India Anthology of Poetry* (1994), *Living in America: Fiction and Poetry by South Asian-American Writers* (1995), *Contours of the Heart* (1996), *Uncommon Wealth* (1997), *Vespers: Contemporary American Poems* of *Religion and Spirituality* (2003), *The Bloodaxe Book of Contemporary Indian Poetry* (2008), and *60 Indian Poets*, Penguin Books (2008). His poetry
continues to appear in journals both in print like *World Literature Today*, *Kavya Bharati, Atlas, Wasafiri*, and in online magazines like *coldnoon.com, muse-india.com, undergroundflowers.com,
sangampoetryhouse.com*, and others. *Ariel* has also featured a long interview with him. *The Oxford Companion to Twentieth Century Poets* (1994) carries an entry on Peeradina.

Peeradina has given readings all over the world. In 2003, he served as writer-in-residence at merican College, Madurai, India, and at Lenoir-Rhyne College, NC. In 2009-10, he was writer-in-residence at The Chelsea Pubic Library, MI.Peeradina is Professor Emeritus at Siena Heights University, Adrian, Michigan.

Shanta Acharya

Shanta Acharya was born and educated in India before studying at Oxford and Harvard. The author of **ten** books, her latest poetry collection is *Dreams That Spell The Light*. Her poems, articles and reviews have appeared in major publications worldwide. **Her** *New & Selected Poems* is due for publication in 2016. She is the **founding** director of Poetry in the House, Lauderdale House in London, where she has been hosting monthly poetry readings since 1996. She has served on the board of trustees of the Poetry Society, The Poetry School and the Arvon Foundation **in the UK**. More information about her work available at:

www.shantaacharya.com

Reginald Massey

Reginald Massey has authored several works on South Asia. His books on the classical dance and music of the subcontinent are required reading for all those who study these subjects. He wrote and produced *Bangladesh I Love You*, a film which starred the boxing phenomenon Muhammad Ali. *Azaadi!*, his collection of stories and histories concerned South Asia after 1947. His poetry collection *Lament of a Lost Hero and Other Poems* chronicles subcontinental society in the post-independence period. His poems have appeared in the following anthologies. His latest books are *INDIA: Definitions and Clarifications* (Hansib, London) and *Shaheed Bhagat Singh and the Forgotten Indian Martyrs* (Abhinav, New Delhi). Among his earlier books was: *All India* (Quintet, London and Quarto, New York). *Asian Dance in Britain* (NRCD, University of Surrey) consisted of a selection of his researches and reviews. He contributed to The Encyclopedia of Dance and Ballet (Edited by Mary Clarke and David Vaughan. Putnams, New York). Massey's obituaries of Indian and Pakistani dancers and musicians have been published in *The Guardian* over the years.

He holds a Masters in English Literature and in 2006 was Visiting Professor of Creative Writing at India's Himachal Pradesh University. Later he was Writer-in-Residence at the Union Bank of Switzerland's think tank at Wolfsberg Chateau, Switzerland. He writes for the Books and Authors section of *DAWN*, the leading national paper of Pakistan. In the United Kingdom he writes for *The Times, The Guardian, The Daily Telegraph* and *The Independent* as well as Confluence and Asian Affairs. He is a senior dance critic for *The Dancing Times*. His novel The Immigrants was well received. He has studied comparative literature and journalism at France's Lille University and is a member of is a member of the Royal Overseas League, the British Society of Authors and is a Fellow of the Royal Society of Arts. Recently he was awarded the Freedom of the City of London.

Usha Akella

Usha Akella is the founder of *The Poetry Caravan* in Austin TX and Greenburg, NY. The Caravan offers readings and workshops to the disadvantaged in women's shelters, senior homes and hospitals.

She has been invited to many international poetry festivals and her work is included in the Harper Collins anthology of poets edited by Sudeep Sen and other anthologies. She has read at reputed organizations as the Omega Institute, NY and Rothko chapel, Houston.

She was awarded the Nazim Hikmet Poetry Prize 2011 by the Siir Festival, Turkey. She was the winner of *Maryland Poetry Review*'s Egan Memorial Contest. She won the informal wine poem award at Struga Poetry Evenings 2006, Macedonia, the first Indian and woman in 45 years to do so.
She was a finalist for the 2010 Pablo Neruda Prize. Her poem 'One hears' was a Pushcart nomination. She received the encourageer of the arts award from the town of Greenburgh, NY.

She has read twice for the Sahitya Academy (considered the highest literary organization in India. She featured with four other poets to represent Indian Writing in English at a 2008 Sahitya Academy poetry event.) She was interviewed on "The Front Row" for NPR/ Houston Public Radio in October 2013. Her poems have appeared in the Sahitya Academy's journal *Indian Literature*.

Her work has appeared and is upcoming in many US and Indian based journals such as *The Bitter Oleander, Drunken Boat, Borderlands, Cumberland Review, The Crab Orchard Review, The Maryland Poetry Review, Pearl, Emily Dickinson Journal, Catamaran, Muse India, Ardent! Di-verse-city, Kavya Bharati* etc.

Usha Kishore

Indian-born Usha Kishore is a British poet, writer and translator from the Sanskrit, resident on the Isle of Man, where she teaches English at Queen Elizabeth II High School. Usha is internationally published and anthologised by *Macmillan, Hodder Wayland, Oxford University Press* (all UK) and *Harper Collins India* among others. Her poetry has won prizes in UK Poetry competitions (the most recent being the winning poem in the *Exiled Writers Ink Poetry Competition)*, has been part of international projects and features in the British Primary and Indian Middle School syllabuses. The winner of an Arts Council Award and a *Culture Vannin* Award, Usha's debut collection *On Manannan's Isle* was published in 2014 by *dpdotcom,*UK. A second collection *Night Sky between the Stars* has been published by *Cyberwit India* in January 2015. Forthcoming is a book of translations from the Sanskrit, *Translations of the Divine Woman,* from *Rasala India*.Currently Usha is translating Kalidasa's_ *tusa_haram.*

****

Sweta Vikram

(Sweta Vikram is our WMP Award winner)
Sweta Srivastava Vikram (www.swetavikram.com), featured by Asian Fusion as 'One of the most influential Asians of our time,' is an award-winning writer, three times Pushcart Prize nominee, Amazon bestselling author of 10 books, novelist, poet, essayist, and columnist. Her latest book, *Wet Silence*, is a full-length collection of poems about Hindu widows. Sweta is also a certified yoga teacher who shares the love and power of yoga with trauma survivors. A graduate of Columbia
University, when Sweta is not doing yoga, cooking, travelling, writing books, or posts for magazines, teaching creative writing, or giving talks on gender

equality, she works as a digital and content marketing consultant. Sweta lives in New York City with her husband and can be found on Twitter [@swetavikram] and Facebook
https://www.facebook.com/Words.By.Sweta

Editor

 **Yogesh Patel**

As a co-editor of Skylark, Yogesh Patel has published international contemporary poetry since the seventies. Currently, he runs Skylark Publications UK and a non-profit **Word Masala** project to promote writers and poets of the South Asian diaspora. Recently he launched a South-Asian 'Poet of the month' e-zine series. Yogesh is also a founder of the *literary charity*, Gujarati Literary Academy, and has served as its president. He was a Fellow of the International Poetry Society and a Fellow of the Royal Society of Arts. He was awarded **the Freedom of the City of London** and has four LP records, two films, radio programmes, children's books, fiction and non-fiction books, including poetry collections to his credit.

Apart from being a recipient of the IWWP award, the International Scottish Diploma for the excellence in poetry, and a Hon. Diploma from the Italian University of Arts, he has won the Co-Op Award for poetry on the environment.

By profession, Yogesh is a qualified optometrist and an accountant.

www.patelyogesh.co.uk

We welcome your comments and support. Please join the list.
8. Please buy the merchandise to help. See our shop at www.skylarkpublictions.co.uk
9. Please subscribe to our crowdfunding projects for the books
10. Please DONATE
11. Please buy our books and the books by our recommended poets
12. Please spread the word about us in your social media
13. PLEASE REVIEW AND PUBLISH OUR DIASPORA POETS
14. Please invite them to events and festivals for the readings and talks.

Acknowledgements

Daljit Nagra: From *Look We Have Coming to Dover!* © Faber and Faber
Debjani Chatterjee's 'Diwali' was published in her collection *Animal Antics* from Pennine Pens, Hebden Bridge.
     Debjani Chatterjee's 'Heart Tanka' was published in her collection *Words Spit and Splinter* from Redbeck Press, Bradford.
     Debjani Chatterjee's 'Victoria's Statues' was published in *On a Camel to the Moon and other poems about journeys* compiled by Valerie Bloom for Belitha Press, London.
     Debjani Chatterjee's 'Winter Tanka', 'Christmas', 'Lotus Meditation', 'UN Observer' and 'The Great Houdini' are previously unpublished.
Meena Alexander: *Inwood Sita*, *Lyric Ego* and *Dwelling* are from a section of the long poem `*Indian Ocean Blues'* from Meena Alexander, *Atmospheric Embroidery* (2015)
     Field in Summer is from *Raw Silk* (2004)
Reginal Massey: All from Lament of a Lost Hero, A Writers Workshop, Calcutta
Saleem Peeradina: Four poems *From* Meditation on Desire, Sisters from *Group Portrait*. Published by Oxford University Press and all others are exclusively from the forthcoming book out in June 2016, Valley Press.
Shanta Acharya: *Christmas Gifts,* was published in two magazines in the UK - *Thumbscrew* and *Confluence*. *Boxing Day*'is from her collection *Dreams That Spell The Light.Fever in Diwali* from *Not This, Not That 'London: 7th July 2005* from *Shringara*
Sweta Vikram:
Usha Kishore: All poems from *On Manannan's Isle, dpdotcom;*
     From Hatred to Love is yet unpublished.
Usha Akella : All poems previously unpublished
Yogesh Patel: All poems previously unpublished

New books by the Word Masala award winners:

'*Night Sky Between the Stars*' **by Usha Kishore** TThe cosmic dance of feminine ceation challenges age-old patriarchal myth of subjecthood in these poems...--
Professor Bashabi Fraser, Edinburgh Napier

ISBN 798-81-8253-566-4, Cyberwit.net
Buy from http://ww.ushakishore.co.uk

'*Atmospheric Embroidery*' **by Meena Alexander**

Meena Alexander is a truth-teller who knows how to make language do anything and everything she desires.
                            -**Yusef Komunyaka**

ISBN 978-93-5195-017-2 Hachette India
Buy from Amzon.co.uk

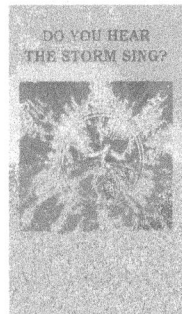

Do You Hear the Storm Sing? By Debjani Chatterjee
What a marvellous title - I'd steal it!
What a lovely cover -I'd kiss it!
And what marvellous poems -I'd plagiarise them!!!
-**Barry Tebb - Poet, Editor and Publisher of Sixties Press**

ISBN 978-0-9573837-5-3 Core Publications
Email orders: coreditions@yahoo.co.uk

Ramayana A Retelling by Daljit Nagra
This is, first, not a faithful retelling but a high-octane mythology redux which makes a conscious effort to be contemporary.
-**Arifa Akbar, The Independent**

ISBN 9780571313846 Buy from **Faber and Faber**

A World Elsewhere, a novel by Shanta Acharya

We are here in the realm of Camus, if with a very different result.

-Lance Lee, Muse India

ISBN 978-1-4917-4364-5 iUniverse
Buy from Amazon.co.uk

Wet Silence by Sweta Vikram
(Our WMP Award winner)
"Sweta Vikram captures bold raw passion, poignant reality and crafts a powerful voice for the voiceless."
-**Kate Campbell Stevenson, Actor & Producer**

ISBN 978-1-61599-256-0 (softcover : acid-free paper)
ISBN 978-1-61599-257-7 (hardcover : acid-free paper)
ISBN 978-1-61599-258-4 (ebook) **Morden History Press**

The Rosary of Latitude by Usha Akella

Usha Akella's The Rosary of Latitudes is an odyssey across lands stretching from Istanbul to Venice to Nicaragua and Mexico, a mix of poetry and prose, of rapture and reality.
-**Keki Daruwala, The Hindu**

ISBN 978 0 9962704 0 3
Buy at http://transcendentzeropress.org/

Saleem Peeradina

Out in June 2016

Valley Press

Help a fellow poet and register your pre-purchase interest at **www.valleypressuk.com**. This also opens a door for you to be considered in future as it is a pre-condition that your buy at least one book from them.

Quote a reference: Saleem Peeradina/Word Masala and they may give you some discount too!

Year's Highlights

Congratulations to Debjani Chatterjee, Shanta Acharya, Usha Akella, Usha Kishore, Meena Alexander and Sweta Vikram for their new collections, anthologies and novels published this Year.

Congratulations to Saleem Peeradina for the acceptance of his new collection by Valley Press to be published in (June) 2016. Some of Saleem's poems published in this annual are from that anthology allowing you to see what you will miss if you don't buy this important collection. Please register your interest direct or with us and pre-order to encourage the poet and the publisher.

Congratulations to Matwaala movement. Organized by Usha Akella, first **Matwaala Literary Festival** shaped up and took place in Austin. Saleem Peeradina and Pramilla Venkateswaran were also instrumental in helping Usha to pull this off as a great and varied cultural event.

Congratulations to Usha Akella for winning the Open Road Review Poetry Prize

Congratulations to Lord Bhikhu Parekh on his new book entitled *Debating India: Essays on Indian Political Discourse* published by Oxford University Press. This book includes a fascinating chapter on brotherly relations in our epics, a unique study on this subject. A must read for all!

Congratulations to Mona Dash on being selected for Word Masala Project's first crowdfunding venture. Mona has already published one collection and has a novel to be published soon. Please contribute now to this subscription publication in advance to help our cause.

**Please support this new initiative.
It could be you in the future!**

Our **successful PR campaign** as poetry on a mug featured in the media and highlighted our cause to important people and organizations.

**Please buy it at our website
to help
Word Masala Not-for-Profit project.**

**Alternatively, for your own PR campaign,
ask us to organize your own poem on a pillow cover,
t-shirt, mobile or laptop covers, light shade and others.
Please ask for a quote.**

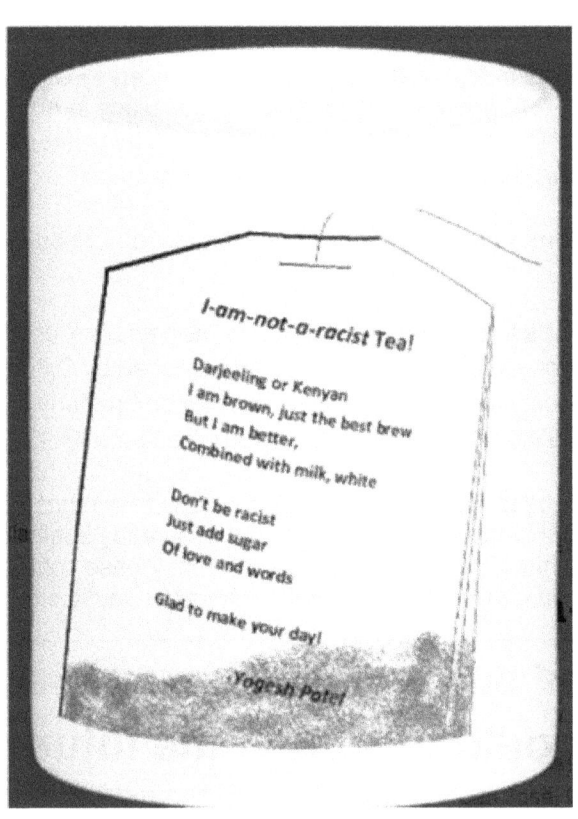

Some examples of main sections from
eSkylark e-zine & magazine

Join the list to support us
editor@skylarkpublications.co.uk

1. You keep up-to-date with new regulations

Attention
Applies to all publishers and authors self-publishing or selling their services

New rules for Online Dispute Resolution due in force from January 2016

From 9 January 2016, all **businesses that sell goods or services online must place a link on their website to the EU Commission's Online Dispute Resolution (ODR) Platform.** Online businesses that are committed to using ADR must also provide information about the ODR platform in their contractual terms and conditions.

From January 2016, the European Commission will set up an online platform (the ODR platform). This will allow consumers who have a complaint about a product or service bought online to submit the complaint via an online complaint form to a trader based in another European country. In cross-border disputes, consumers needing assistance in filling out the form and traders receiving a complaint will be able to get information and assistance from advisers based in their own country, who will work with their European counterparts to facilitate communication between the parties involved in the dispute.

From 9 January 2016, all online traders must provide a link to the ODR platform on their website and state the online trader's e-mail address, irrespective of whether they currently market their products or services to consumers in other Member States. An online marketplace must provide a link to the ODR platform on its website.

Where, under an enactment, trade association rules or a term of a contract, a trader is obliged to use an ADR procedure provided by an ADR entity or EU listed body, the trader must, in addition, provide a link to the ODR platform in any offer made to a consumer by e-mail and inform consumers of the existence of the ODR platform and the possibility of using the ODR platform for resolving disputes. This information must also be provided in general online terms and conditions for sales or services contracts where they exist.

(Article by courtesy of Federation of Small Businesses)

2. **You keep up-to-date with new reviews and get reviewed if join the Review Group**

Reviews

A Review Group

Word Masala has set up a review group. We want to develop this group. The practical position in the publishing world is that if you are not prepared to review books by other poets and authors, it will be wrong to expect others to review your books. Reviewing takes time and effort. If everyone thinks it is a waste of time, then we will have a continued problem. If you are not pro-active in creating helpful conditions, then more and more publishers will ignore diaspora writers. They may not be in it for the money, but they also need to survive. So let us feed their marketing with something that we can do proactively. Please write to us to participate as much as you can to this group. Debjani Chatterjee, Saleem Peeradina and Reginald Massey were among the first to make this exchange a reality.

May I also I request readers to buy the books by our diasporic poets? Just read some reviews here to get an idea of the books by these poets. Thanks.

-Editor

ISBN 978-0-9573837-5-3   Core Publications

Dr Marium Nesha reviews Dabjani Chatterjee's *Do You Hear the Storm Sing*?

Debjani Chatterjee, *Do You Hear the Storm Sing*? London, Core Publications, 2014, 73pp, ISBN: 978-0-9573837-5-3, price: £8.99.

Debjani Chatterjee is a prolific writer and Britain's best-known Asian poet. Her latest collection lives up to my every expectation. There are poems here that move me beyond words. And yet, in reviewing this book, I must try to find some words.

These poems bring a burst of Indian sunshine to cheer the winter's gloom in Britain. They travel the world and come like jewels from India, Britain, Japan, China, Palestine, Pakistan and elsewhere. In a poem that I would strongly recommend, 'Salaam, My Poet-Friends', the dust in a graveyard proclaims that it knows no boundaries:

> Freely I flow between Lahore and Ambala,
> Freely I fly through Delhi, Sheffield and Kolkata;
> I need no passport for Jerusalem and Ramalla.

The poetry of this much-travelled writer is similarly global in scope and claims the same freedom.

There are frolicsome poems like 'Drink Conundrum' that reflect her gift for humour:

> Otters on water are frisky;
> People on whisky are risky.

Then there are serious poems that convey a profound message. As I write this in the wake of the terrorist massacres in Paris, the lesson of 'Here At Mamilla' rings with particular urgency:

> the Prophet's Sahabah, Sufis, soldiers
> of Saladin, crusaders, high and low,
> lie equal in the rhythm of history.
> ....
> Our peace too depends on their middle ground.

Other poems that especially speak to me are the many exploring relationships, motherhood and the experiences of travel, exile and migration. Among these I would single out: 'Home Is Where The Heart Is' and 'An Asian Child Enters A British Classroom'. The latter is a telling comment on the two or more worlds that the child of immigrants must inhabit: an Asian schoolgirl enters her classroom by shedding her 'language, name, identity' as she prepares 'for lessons in cultural anonymity'.

Debjani Chatterjee's 'cancer' poems touch on a difficult subject and do so with great feeling. 'What I Did Today' is a poem that empowers every patient who has suffered trauma and neglect in encounters with medical professionals; while the four haiku of 'Rafts of Hope' are an uplifting anthem for the whole 'survivor' movement.

he author has a gift for haiku and tanka; these often appear in deceptively simple language. 'My Cup Of Tea', a tanka containing a haiku in the first three lines, is one of my favourites:

> Both hands cup my mug,
> as I sip my future dreams,
> swirling their contents.
>
> My cup runneth over with
> rich liquid satisfaction.

Like all Bengalis, I love my rice and can echo the words of 'Amma Says...'

> cutlery is silly
> ....
> Eating rice
> is quicker and tastier with one's hands.
> Food should be seen, smelt
> and touched to be truly tasted.

I recommend that this delightful book of poems *Do You Hear the Storm Sing?* should also be truly tasted.

Dr Marium Nesha

A member of the Healing Word and Bengali Women's Support Group, Dr Marium Nesha has contributed to several anthologies, e.g. Barbed Lines, Sweet & Sour, and A Slice of Sheffield.

ISBN 798-81-8253-566-4 Cyberwit.net

Mona Dash reviews *'Night Sky Between the Stars'* **by Usha Kishore**
Usha Kishore, *Night Sky Between the Stars* India, Cyberwit.net, 2015, 108pp, ISBN: 978-81-8253-566-4, price: £7.99.

'Night Sky Between The Stars' is Usha Kishore's second collection of poetry, with fifty-five poems in total. It includes two sets of Ekphrastic poetry; Gendered Yearnings, based on the paintings of Raja Ravi Verma, one of the greatest painters in the history of Indian Art and the second set Prerna, in association with Indian artist Sandhya Arvind, who uses the indigenous Warli and Madhubani repertoires.

The poems are largely based on Indian myth, exploring shades and nuances of various mythological characters – Draupadi 'What if I am the beloved of the Pandavas?' praying to Krishna to 'Clothe me from eternity to eternity'; Gandhari, 'Blindfolded, I view the world, wedded to a nation of blind men' laments 'Cursed woman that I am'; or Sita, 'you are the earth waiting for the sky' being told 'Banish him, as he banished you.'

The poems draw in many instances from Sanskrit verse, and this is only natural considering that Kishore is also a Sanskrit scholar. The title poem, for example, 'Night Sky Between the Stars' is inspired by Kalidasa. It explores womanhood in all her forms;

I am she – cosmic soul, dark warrior,
Fecund earth, making love to the sky.
My endless female hungers pouring
out in universes that I laboriously
carry in my womb.

Other poems in the collection explore myths such as the 'Girl Trees', dedicated to the women of Piplantari in Rajasthan, India, a village where, very surprisingly, a tree is planted every time a girl is born. 'Mother Earth reborn, every girl becomes a tree, every tree a girl.' And in sharp contrast to it, 'Fairies Hanging' is poignant and chilling at the same time, 'For in my India, they flay fairies and hang them on mango trees.'

Kishore's previous collection On Manannan's isle and many of her poems, in general, are nostalgic, dreamily exploring the culture and world she has left behind, in contrast to the world she has embraced and now lives in. Some of the poems in this collection take this theme forward. In 'Translated Woman', an adaptation of Rushdie's phrase translated man, Kishore says
'My insides are a tug of war
Between East and West,
Who keep their trysts in darkness;
They have met and courted somewhere
And now live together in sin.
 I am their progeny'
………………………………

I am the brushstroke of Ravi Varma, dipped in Monet's colours.
I am a translated woman.'

In L'Ecriture Feminine et Indienne, Kishore declares 'Toutes mes langues sont colonials. Elle sont les enfants terribles de la polotique.' (All my languages are colonial/They are the terrible children of politics.)

The collection is varied; with some of the poems steeped in Indian philosophy and spirituality, and drawing on Sanskrit to flavour them; and others exploring culture, myths, inequalities, womanhood heightened, diaspora, tradition. All along Kishore uses her trademark choice of expressions, words which immediately take you to the world she comes from and she wants to see; poems tempered with her strong sense of language and imagery.
Indeed, with this collection, Kishore adorns the literary sky with many stars.

3. **Once a year we choose a poet for our _subscription publishing._**
We will not consider anyone who has not subscribed to this initiative.
PLEASE go to our website and support this
Only £9.99

http://www.skylarkpublications.co.uk/crowdfunding.html

A collection by poet Mona Dash

A Competition

When you subscribe in advance for the publication of Mona Dash's book, please don't forget to suggest a title based on a proposed book cover shown here. A panel of judges from our Word Masala Award will pick a winner. Here is a teaser for it:
'*My Blue Tree*'..?

Mona Dash will compose a poem with a winning title in mind which will be included in the book. The poem will be dedicated to the winner.

To appreciate further, with a copy of the book, the winner also will receive a mug featuring own photograph on it.

So, will you still not support this subscription publication?

4. **You keep up-to-date with new FEE FREE Awards and competitions every month**

Our Awards

Word Masala Awards are only conferred on published South-Asian diaspora poets with a substantial quality and quantity of work that confirm their achievements are of the highest standards. They are a 'Lifetime Achievement'. We look for a wide range of subject matter offered, and consider the poet's recognisable contribution to literature, including any special achievements. All our past winners, we are very proud to say, meet these criteria. Only these winners are invited to contribute to the winners' anthology published by Skylark Publications UK. These winners will also nominate and help us in our consultations for future nominations. We do hope that our winners will help fellow diaspora poets where possible, and take an active interest in this project through mentoring, reviewing, helping with a preface, providing comments for blurbs, helping to judge competitions, etc. Winners are also expected to include a mention of the award in their bio-data and to link their page at www.skylarkpublications.co.uk to their blogs, social media platforms and webpages.

Others may receive **WMP Special Citation Certificate Awards**. For example, a citation can be for being an 'activist poet' or an 'emerging voice'. Our website will display such citations.

All the above mentioned award winners and other generally featured poets may quote our **Honour bestowed on them as Poet-of-the-Month.**

In future, we intend to add **Word Masala Poetry in Translation Awards** as we start featuring the translation of well-known diaspora poets writing in the mother tongue. A separate anthology will be published to celebrate their work.work.

After you win any of our Awards, *you are* NOT FORGOTTEN. Our support is non-stop.

Marketing that may cost you hundreds of pounds, if not thousands, is freely given to the winners.

For more information visit www.skylarkpublications.co.uk

5. You keep up-to-date with some important news and articles

Junot Diaz On Why It's So Important To Read Authors Who Don't Look Like You
http://www.huffingtonpost.com/entry/junot-diaz-breaks-down-the-importance-of-reading-authors-from-diverse-backgrounds_560edbbae4b0af3706e0c355

Rushdie: Publishers front line in free speech battle
http://www.thebookseller.com/news/rushdie-publishers-front-line-free-speech-battle-314318

6. You keep up-to-date with Markets

Call for Submissions: Poet's Market 2017
http://www.writersdigest.com/whats-new/call-for-submissions-poets-market-2017

Upstreet Literary Journal
Submission period: September 1, 2015-March 1, 2016. Award-winning literary annual *upstreet* seeks quality submissions of short fiction, creative nonfiction, and poetry for its twelfth issue.
http://www.upstreet-mag.org/submissions/

7. You keep up-to-date with Free Compettions

RESTLESS BOOKS PRIZE, NO ENTRY FEE.
http://www.restlessbooks.com/prize-for-new-immigrant-writing
The Restless Books Prize for New Immigrant Writing will alternate yearly between accepting unpublished fiction and nonfiction submissions, beginning with fiction in 2015. Fiction submissions can take the form of a novel or a collection of short stories. Nonfiction submissions can take the form of a memoir, a collection of essays, or a book-length work of narrative nonfiction. Candidates must be first-generation residents of the United States. "First-generation" can refer either to people born in another country who relocated to the U.S., or to American-born residents whose parents were born elsewhere. Candidates must not have previously published a book in English. The winner will receive a $10,000 advance and publication by Restless Books in print and digital editions. Deadline December 31, 2015. *(Reprinted with courtesy of their website)*

8. You keep up-to-date with Publishing updates

Amazon has expanded its Kindle Scout crowd-sourcing publishing programme to the UK.

The programme was launched in the US last October and has been rolled out to other countries in Europe, Canada, Australia, New Zealand, South Africa, Mexico, Brazil, Japan and India, among others.

Amazon described the platform as "reader-powered", allowing authors to submit manuscripts and be considered for publication in 45 days or less under Amazon's digital publishing banner Kindle Press.

Publishing contracts include five-year renewable terms, a $1,500 (£975) advance, a 50% e-book royalty rate, easy rights reversions and featured Amazon marketing the company said.

Dina Hilal, general manager of Kindle Scout, said: "Expanding our platform to authors and readers outside the US has been one of the most frequent requests we've received since we launched. With today's announcement, we're eagerly awaiting the great new stories that will come from opening to even more talented writers and Scouts from around the world."

Amazon said that through the Kindle Scout programme, 75 titles had been selected for publication by Kindle Press, with Kindle Press books receiving an average Amazon Customer Review of 4.48 stars across 2,709 reviews.

Under the terms of Kindle Scout, books have 30 days to earn a nomination from a reader. Readers can nominate up to three books at a time and they will receive an email to inform them whether the book has been selected for publication. Readers who nominate books that are published will receive an early, free copy.

9. And events, audio, poetry films, and more.

We announce a celebration of our winners at

the House of Lords

on 22nd June 2016.

Editors and publishers who wish to support us are welcome to request an invitation

www.ingramcontent.com/pod-product-compliance
Lightning Source LLC
Chambersburg PA
CBHW071415040426
42444CB00009B/2253